INSTITUTE

SU ...ES

ilm

...ase

Published for the
Institute of Leadership & Management by

Pergamon
Flexible
Learning

OXFORD   AMSTERDAM   BOSTON   LONDON   NEW YORK   PARIS
SAN DIEGO   SAN FRANCISCO   SINGAPORE   SYDNEY   TOKYO

Pergamon Flexible Learning
An imprint of Elsevier Science
Linacre House, Jordan Hill, Oxford OX2 8DP
200 Wheeler Road, Burlington, MA 01803

First published 1986
Second edition 1991
Third edition 1997
Fourth edition 2003

British Library Cataloguing in Publication Data
A catalogue record for this book is available from the British Library

ISBN 0 7506 5892 4

For information on Pergamon Flexible Learning
visit our website at www.bh.com/pergamonfl

Institute of Leadership & Management
registered office
1 Giltspur Street
London
EC1A 9DD
Telephone 020 7294 3053
www.i-l-m.com
ILM is part of the City & Guilds Group

The views expressed in this work are those of the authors and do
not necessarily reflect those of the Institute of Leadership &
Management or of the publisher

Authors: Clare Donnelly and Raymond Taylor
Editor: Clare Donnelly
Editorial management: Genesys, www.genesys-consultants.com
Composition by Genesis Typesetting Limited, Rochester, Kent
Printed and bound in Great Britain by MPG Books, Bodmin

Contents

Contents

Workbook introduction

1 ILM Super Series study links

This workbook addresses the issues of *Making a Financial Case*. Should you wish to extend your study to other Super Series workbooks covering related or different subject areas, you will find a comprehensive list at the back of this book.

2 Links to ILM Qualifications

This workbook relates to the following learning outcomes in segments from the ILM Level 3 Introductory Certificate in First Line Management and the Level 3 Certificate in First Line Management.

C4.7   Cost/benefit analysis
1   Identify an example of change in the organization
2   List items of capital cost which may arise
3   List areas where net savings may be achieved
4   Identify wider non-financial implications
5   Understand the principles of payback or other simple means of investment appraisal

3 Links to S/NVQs in Management

This workbook relates to the following elements of the Management Standards which are used in S/NVQs in Management, as well as a range of other S/NVQs.

A1.3   Make recommendations for improvements to work activities
B1.1   Make recommendations for the use of resources

It will also help you to develop the following Personal Competences:

- communicating;
- thinking and taking decisions;
- focusing on results.

4 Workbook objectives

In our daily lives we need to decide how to spend our money and set priorities. Do we buy the latest home entertainment system or is it better to take our family on holiday? It would be good if we could do both but there is usually not enough money to go around.

Businesses and non-profit-making organizations have the same problem. If a business buys a machine which is the most efficient on the market and will give it a competitive advantage, this will add to profit, which will benefit owners and shareholders. But perhaps the purchase means deferring a pay rise for employees and will lead to unrest. In spending money the business must make choices and weigh the costs and benefits of each option.

Some choices are more difficult than others. A hospital may have enough money available to buy a foetal monitor which will help save the lives of, say, a dozen babies a year; or a kidney dialysis machine which will save 300 older people a year having to travel fifty miles to the next available dialysis centre. Which would you choose?

We need to have criteria against which we can make decisions like these, and ways to measure the potential advantages and disadvantages of using resources available to us. And, because money is limited, you, as a first line manager, need the skills to be able to ensure that you have a good chance of receiving a fair share of the funds available. To say: 'We need £20,000 for a new piece of equipment' is not enough. You need to justify why **you** should receive the money and not someone in another department.

In this workbook we will look at ways of evaluating projects in financial, and other, terms and how to prepare a financial case.

4.1 Objectives

When you have completed this workbook you will be better able to:

■ understand the ways in which changes and ideas develop into projects;
■ use techniques to appraise investment;
■ prepare a financial case.

5 Activity planner

If you are compiling an S/NVQ portfolio, you might like to develop some of the Activities in this workbook as the basis of possible evidence of your competence. They are all marked with the 'Portfolio of evidence' icon shown on the left. Particular Activities you may want to look at in advance are:

■ Activity 6: which asks you to perform SWOT and PESTLE analyses;
■ Activity 11: where you examine relevant past experience in making a financial case for change;
■ Activities 22 and 25: where you will explore your organization's relevant financial policies and procedures, in preparation for Activity 26;
■ Activity 26: where you look at appraising equipment that is due for replacement;
■ Activity 29: where you undertake a payback and return on investment exercise;
■ Activity 30: which invites you to look at your own organization's procedures for presenting a case.

The Work-based assignment suggests that you speak to your manager, finance director or to your colleagues in the accounts office about the way in which you should go about making a case for finance or a share of the budget in your organization. You might like to start thinking now about whom to approach and arrange to speak with them.

Session A
Changes, ideas and projects

1 Introduction

You will be regularly faced with decisions about **changes** at home, such as whether to buy a new three-piece suite or a multimedia computer to help you and your partner or children better understand the new technology and improve future work prospects. What influences you to think about these changes in the first place? And what makes you have these particular options, where other people may choose between a replacement car or a holiday in similar circumstances?

Everyone has different needs, wants and tastes. In each case, something needs to be satisfied. And it is the same in organizations, the managers and owners of which will want to improve service, enhance profits and ensure survival.

In organizations there are likely to be a number of individuals, all with their own **ideas** about how changes will improve matters for themselves and their customers. Perhaps you would like new equipment to help you and your workteam be more effective, or would like to see more money spent on training to improve the productivity of your team? Ideally senior managers will undertake thorough analysis of these ideas and prioritize the options to ensure that the best use is made of resources available, and ideas are turned into effective **projects**.

In this session we will look at how ideas arise from changes, why some are given greater attention than others, and why some are finally turned into viable projects and others are not. By understanding what makes a project viable in your organization, you will be better able to appreciate what those who authorize the spending of money are looking for.

2 Identifying changes in the organization

As a first line manager you have your ear very 'close to the ground' with regard to what is going on in your organization.

Activity 1   3 mins

How do you think your position as first line manager puts you in an excellent position for spotting changes in the organization?

_____

_____

You probably came up with a range of factors:

■ Contact with customers – so you know whether or not they are satisfied, and whether they are asking for new products and services which you are currently not providing.

■ Contact with staff engaged in day-to-day operations – so you know whether they are happy or frustrated, whether they need more training or better conditions, whether they are tempted to join competitors or believe they are already in the best organization.

■ Contact with suppliers making deliveries and taking returns – so you know what they can do well and what they do badly, and have some idea of new products or services they are offering, or new customers they have taken on who are competitors of yours.

■ Contact with competitors at trade fairs or 'on the road' – so you have the latest gossip on their staff, finances, products and services, technology and future plans.

These types of information are vital to any organization. It needs to keep up with the pace of developments in the world around it, or what we can call its overall 'external environment', and the constant developments within itself, or what we can call its 'internal environment'.

But remember that the information you pick up about changes is probably confined to the operational level of the organization. Of course changes also take place at higher levels of management, such as:

- at the tactical level, where middle managers may pick up on an opportunity to form an alliance with a major supplier, or a joint venture with a competitor;
- at the strategic level, where the most senior managers may have to cope with a major change in technology or markets, or may have to refinance the business due to a fall in the stock markets.

Activity 2

3 mins

Try to think of a recent change that has affected you and your workteam. It may be an increase in staff numbers, a new procedure or product, a new piece of equipment or a change in working times.

Who first suggested the change?

_____

Where do you think the impetus for the change came from?

_____

Was the change brought about because of developments in the **external** environment or because of ideas in the **internal** environment, or a combination of the two?

_____

Even if you were the first person to suggest the change, because of your knowledge and experience 'at the coalface', it is unlikely that a change of any size would be successfully implemented without the support of your immediate manager and possibly of other managers as well. The impetus for seeing change through is often a team effort on the part of the management group.

As to whether changes are the result of internal or external forces, you may have struggled to identify this point. In the next section we will look at a few techniques for analysing the forces for change which will help us here.

The important point, however, is that some changes are unavoidable – they are effectively imposed by forces which cannot be withstood. This is particularly the case with changes caused by legislation or regulations, and changes caused by economic or market forces.

2.1 The need to make a financial case for change

Where a change is needed, or an idea is developed that requires a change, you and/or your senior manager will need more resources to make that change effectively. As we saw in Activity 2, these resources may be an increase in staff numbers or a new piece of equipment, both of which obviously require extra resources in the form of money.

But what about other changes – do these require resources?

Activity 3

What resources are needed for the following changes to be implemented effectively?

A new procedure or product

_____

A change in working times

_____

Well, introducing a new procedure or product nearly always requires some staff training, which requires the resources of money (to pay for the training cost, say) and time. And implementing a change in working times may mean taking on some part-time staff to cover for gaps, or the payment of some sort of bonus for the inconvenience involved, or the subsidy of transport costs if staff have to travel home late at night.

What we are concentrating on here are the **costs** of change. Clearly there must also be some **benefits**, otherwise there would be no point in making the change. So when you are trying to persuade 'the powers that be' that a change should be made, you need to put forward a case based on the financial costs and benefits as well as the operational costs and benefits. Ideally the financial benefits will be greater than the financial costs, so your organization can profit from change.

Sometimes, though, a change will result in a net cost. An example is where a change has been imposed by, say, regulations. Then the only (non-financial) benefit may be the knowledge that the organization has acted in compliance with what is legally required.

In such cases, the financial case you are making is not so much for **whether** the change should be made, but rather for **how** it should be made at the least cost and maximum effectiveness.

Where changes are discretionary – that is, they are much more a matter of genuine choice, between maintaining things as they are, or making a change – then the financial case will be to present the change in terms of its overall financial and non-financial benefits.

We shall see in the next session that this distinction affects how the financial evaluation of costs and benefits is made. In this session we shall concentrate on what leads to changes.

3 The forces for change

Most projects for which you will be making a financial case will be directly associated with your immediate workplace. And the ideas leading to projects will come from changes in working practices.

Activity 4 · 2 mins

Write down **two** changes which have meant expenditure on projects in your workplace.

_____

_____

There are a number of possibilities you may have suggested. Among them may be:

- new health and safety regulations necessitating new safety equipment;
- new contracts requiring the purchase of specialist machinery;
- general technological developments improving efficiency and productivity;
- the impact of competition from rivals.

3.1 SWOT analysis

As circumstances change, organizations must change to ensure that they survive and grow. They may undertake a SWOT analysis from time to time which means identifying:

S trengths   and capitalizing on them
W eaknesses   and limiting the effect of them
O pportunities   and making the most of them
T hreats   and taking action against them.

Activity 5

6 mins

CD Productions specializes in reproducing compact discs (CDs) for the music industry. It is a small manufacturing organization with limited funds but has a reputation for quality products and good contacts with other production companies.

The marketing department's projections for the digital video disc (DVD) suggest that the music industry will be producing all new albums on DVD within five years, although there is a chance that take up of DVD technology will never match that of CDs.

CD Productions does not have the finance to buy DVD reproduction equipment at present.

Identify the Strengths, Weaknesses, Opportunities and Threats posed by this situation. How should CD Productions react to the situation?

_____

_____

_____

_____

_____

A SWOT analysis should have drawn out the following:

- Strengths – reputation and contacts, established technology;
- Weaknesses – lack of finance and equipment;
- Opportunities – possible long-term viability of CDs over DVD;
- Threats – going out of business.

As the only opportunity relates to the *chance* that CDs will survive, there is limited action that CD Productions can take in a situation like this. It could use its reputation and contacts and sell out its expertise in the music business to 'friendly' competition; wait in the hope that DVD production equipment becomes cheaper or that DVDs do not sell; or try to create a niche market in specialist CDs for those who continue to use the older technology. Perhaps the business could build an export market.

You may have suggested any of the above and perhaps thought through more than one option. This is a good example of how changed circumstances lead to ideas which need to be explored. CD Productions needs to fight for survival and the organization cannot afford to ignore the future.

EXTENSION 1
Take a look at Part II for more information on PESTLE and SWOT.

SWOT analysis focuses on the strengths as well as weaknesses of an organization.

3.2 PESTLE analysis

PESTLE analysis considers the following influences

P olitical   such as the privatization of British Rail and the subsequent fate of Railtrack
E conomic   factors like low inflation and interest rates
S ocial   matters like the impact of the Internet
T echnological   improvements like digital broadcasting
L egal   issues such as the Working Time Directive
E nvironmental matters such as emission control and 'polluter pays'.

The factors can be either beneficial or disadvantageous.

Activity 6

S/NVQ A1.3, B1.1

Use of natural materials and creation of a caring image developed a strong niche market for the Body Shop. Retail multiples reacted by adopting a similar environmentally friendly approach.

This Activity may provide the basis of appropriate evidence for your S/NVQ portfolio. If you are intending to take this course of action, it might be better to write your answers on separate sheets of paper.

Think about the products or services which your workteam produces or delivers (select no more than three). Perform SWOT and PESTLE analyses on them.

Identify and make notes about areas where change seems inevitable.

_____

_____

_____

_____

_____

_____

_____

_____

_____

_____

_____

_____

_____

If you are compiling an S/NVQ portfolio you may be able to develop your notes into a full report about necessary changes to provide to management. You may be able to use your report and feedback on it as the basis of possible acceptable evidence.

You may have identified changes in standards required by the European Union (EU), or a need to develop niche markets because cheaper imports are damaging sales. Or perhaps social changes, such as people taking more holidays abroad where they have seen higher standards of service, are meaning changes in customer relations in your industry. No matter what industry you are working in, change is likely to be on the horizon.

Having analysed the forces for change and thought about them and the possibilities for the future, the next step is to design and develop ideas for how opportunities are to be exploited and threats are to be countered. Then, of course, the developed idea needs to be implemented as a project.

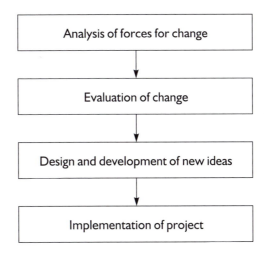

A major part of this process is knowing **when** changes need to be made. No doubt you have experienced situations when, in hindsight, changes have been made too early or too late. Experience, good instincts and practice will help you identify the best time to make changes. This is an important management skill.

4 Time for change

Some organizations welcome change. Others are forced into it. Certain organizations seem to have been in the right place at the right time. Any manager who can spot not only the need for change but also get the timing right is a valuable asset.

Activity 7 · 6 mins

Look at the following examples and say if you think it is the right time for change. (Encircle your answer.) Give a brief reason for your answer.

1   A product which is built by hand has been on the market for a few years. Many more people are interested in purchasing it and have the money to buy.

The organization is considering bringing in new automated production techniques.

Is it time for change?   YES/NO

_____

_____

2   Branch banking services have been provided by most banks for many years and have become increasingly expensive to run. They are not effective in retaining and gaining customers and the value of the premises owned has risen in recent years. A bank is considering selling its branches and offering telephone, postal and computer banking from a few regional centres.

Is it time for change?   YES/NO

_____

_____

3   Massive investment in new plant and machinery has been made by an organization to take advantage of a potential new market which has not materialized. It cost £100,000 and only £15,000 has been generated from sales. A further £15,000 is expected in the next year and then £10,000 a year for another five years after that.

Is it time for change?   YES/NO

_____

_____

1   A new, potentially strong market is growing and it is now time for change to take advantage of this. Such an opportunity was spotted by Henry Ford when he set up one of the first production lines. Unfortunately, further suggestions for changes to improve gearboxes, transmissions, engines and hydraulic brakes were turned down and Ford lost its lead to General Motors.

The time for change may not be just one time but all the time.

2 This again appears to be time for change, to take advantage of new opportunities in technology, and the motive may be to stay ahead or keep up with competition.

However, the bank has to be sure of its ground. Do customers really want technology and no 'friendly face'? Branch closures are often very unpopular. It may be time for **a** change, but not for the closure of branches on a grand scale. Sometimes change must be done slowly.

3 It is difficult to think of change, having spent a lot of money and not seen a good return. However, if other opportunities exist which will provide a better return on the money spent, change should be made.

The £100,000 spent on the plant and machinery is a **sunk** cost, expenditure which has been made and is now past. When looking at future opportunities you should not try to include a recovery of past mistakes in your calculations.

4.1 The life cycle

The best times to make change are at clearly defined stages of the life cycle of a product or service.

■ Introduction

The design may need to be altered to meet customer needs. Staff training in all aspects will be required, products will need careful control to avoid over-production or under-production to meet market needs, and distribution and marketing will need to be developed. All of these changes will lead to investment in human resources, equipment and marketing.

■ Growth

More highly productive ways of producing and delivering the product or service, to counteract competitive pressures of entrants into the marketplace, will be the target of investment.

■ Maturity

Market share becomes difficult to increase or even keep. Investment will be geared to niche markets and marketing.

■ Decline

The organization will look for new ideas and needs to decide when to drop a product or service.

You and your workteam will feel the effects of change from each of these stages.

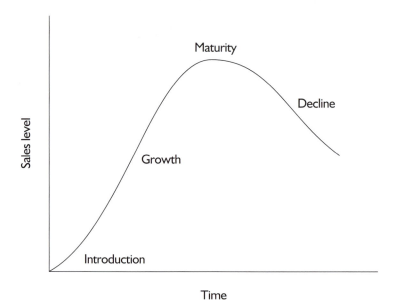

Activity 8 ·

3 mins

Kerry is the floor manager of a high street multiple store selling women's clothing. Her company has decided to introduce a store credit card.

Suggest **two** possible consequences of this for Kerry and her workteam.

_____

_____

You may have identified the need for staff training in the use of the new card. And new equipment and documentation may be needed for the new credit card. Staff will need to become familiar with these.

EXTENSION 2
Various aspects of change are discussed in this very accessible book.

Providing customers with credit cards is likely to increase sales and, perhaps, the volume of customers. This may place extra stress on staff and perhaps lead to sickness and absenteeism. Kerry will need to prepare for these changes, which could affect her budget for staff and training.

You may be faced with similar situations. The more you can predict changes, the easier it will be for you to implement strategies to cope with them and be aware of their possible consequences. This will mean you will be clearer about potential costs and their impact on the resources under your control, so when you need to make a financial case, you will be less likely to overlook anything.

5 How are projects selected?

Have you ever had what you saw as being a good idea and not had it taken forward by your management? Do you know why?

Hopefully you were given feedback and appreciate better why senior managers did not want to spend money on the idea at the time or why it did not fit in the overall plans of the organization. But you may have spent some time working out your idea and felt frustrated at the lack of response.

All projects arise from ideas but not all ideas make it to project stage, especially when the proposed change is not vital, as opposed to unavoidable. Let's have a look at the the process of project evolution so that you will better appreciate whether to spend time developing an idea or not. Putting an idea aside early is just part of evaluating the viability of projects.

Activity 9

5 mins

Peter and Ken Browning are jobbing builders with a reasonably successful small business which earns the partners a profit of about £25,000 each annually from a turnover of £120,000.

Which of the following would be discretionary projects that the partners might consider? (Encircle your answers.) Briefly explain the reasons for your answer.

1   Erecting a double garage for £4000.   Yes/No

_____

2   Building a 200 space supermarket car park for £2,000,000.   Yes/No

_____

3   Resurfacing the flat standing space outside a school for physically
    disabled children, without charge. This is about one day's work.   Yes/No

_____

1   Erecting the double garage seems to be a job well within the capabilities of the partners and this is a discretionary project which the business would consider.

2   You should appreciate that the car park is a major construction project and is likely to be beyond the capabilities, financially and physically, of this partnership.

3   You may equally have said that Peter and Ken Browning would or would not consider the resurfacing job. There is clearly no profit in this option so financially the project does not appear to be viable. But the partners may consider, for charitable reasons, or for the publicity that it attracts, that the project is worth taking on. In taking on such a project, its 'value' is considered with regard to the overall plans of the organization.

As you can see, certain discretionary projects can clearly be turned down because they are beyond what a business would usually contemplate. Small jobbing builders would not have the experience, equipment or labour available to build a car park. And, in the unlikely situation of the partners being given this job, the business would probably run out of money well before the car park was built. Indeed, taking on overly ambitious projects commonly leads to the failure of small businesses. It might, of course, be possible to join together with a consortium of other businesses to take on larger projects. Large construction projects such as the Channel Tunnel are often built and financed by a number of organizations, to spread risk and expertise.

Other jobs are well within the usual day-to-day work and, providing timing is right, a business would carry them out.

We will look at financial techniques for evaluating projects in the next session but you have seen that viability can be measured in ways other than purely financial ones. A larger organization than the Browning partnership might have a specific budget for charitable work and to benefit local communities.

We now effectively have a first-stage set of criteria by which organizations select ideas and consider them for projects.

- Does the organization have to undertake the project, or is it discretionary? Assuming it is discretionary, further criteria must be applied.
- Has the organization the experience to deal with the project?
- Does the organization have the physical resources to carry the project forward?
- Is there the financial muscle to see the project through?
- Has the organization time within its other work to complete the project on schedule?
- Does the project fit within the organization's plans?

If the answer to any of these questions is 'no', the project is unlikely to be considered viable.

Projects can be offered to organizations or can come from within. The above criteria apply both to external and internal opportunities.

6 What can go wrong?

Most people have made plans which have not gone quite as they would have wished. Perhaps a holiday is delayed because of bad weather at the airport. This leads to additional costs for tea, coffee, amusement and, perhaps, hotel bills.

In organizations, things do not always go according to plan. Remember this when you are making a financial case. Senior managers prefer to be given advance warning of possible difficulties rather than continual reports of problems and additional costs after a project has been implemented. A bottleneck in one department may seem a small problem to those in that department but if it affects everyone else in the organization it is not surprising that senior managers become upset.

Activity 10   2 mins

A new computerized invoicing system failed to work effectively, which led to a delay of two weeks in invoicing customers for £520,000 worth of work. This led to extra overdraft interest for the business because of the two-week delay in receiving money.

Assuming 10 per cent interest per annum was charged on the overdraft, calculate the cost. Use the following formula.

$$\frac{\text{Amount invoiced}}{52 \text{ weeks}} \times \text{delay (in weeks)} \times 10\% = \text{Cost}$$

$$\times \qquad \times \qquad =$$

You should have calculated the cost as:

$$\frac{£520,000}{52 \text{ weeks}} \times 2 \times 10\% = £2,000$$

Almost all problems have an identifiable financial cost, although an unpredicted success may have financial benefits.

Typical problems which arise with projects are:

■ implementation taking longer than expected

An example would be computer software not being compatible with existing systems, and the need to improve the ability of the organization's computers to 'talk to each other'.

- major unforeseen problems occurring

  such as a shelter for the homeless being run by a charity attracting people from other areas of the city. This could lead to the facility being unable to provide sufficient food and accommodation for everyone.

- unpredictable external events occurring

  a new butcher's shop facing a renewed scare about brain disease in cows being transmissible to humans.

- short-term crises and competing activities deflecting efforts within the organization

  For example, a health centre may be unable to provide well-man and well-woman clinics if a major flu epidemic occurs, requiring additional resources to be temporarily diverted.

- poor co-ordination

  such as where markets are identified and production increased without an adequate distribution network being set up.

  Well-run organizations need good planning, with appropriate targets and forecasts and proper control. The plans need in-built tolerance levels to allow for some difficulties. Tolerance means the agreed level by which you recognize that performance, and therefore costs, are likely to vary from what is planned.

  When preparing cases for projects, you should not assume that everything will run smoothly. However, any tolerances should be based on experience and reflect a well-planned operation.

  Remember that financial commitments may be major and you should bear in mind the danger of obsolescence, a common problem in industries where there are rapid changes in technology. Watch also for the dangers of particular arrangements. If you suggest changes in fixed assets, like equipment, which are implemented, this may limit further changes. For instance, printers who invested heavily in a litho press for short-run work would be unable to compete in the market with Docutech printers, but also would be unable to raise new finance to invest in Docutech machines themselves.

  In addition, any licensing agreements, agreements with labour, suppliers and competitors can limit future opportunities for change.

Activity 11 · 30 mins

S/NVQ B1.1

This activity may provide the basis of appropriate evidence for your S/NVQ portfolio. If you are intending to take this course of action, it might be better to write your answers on separate sheets of paper.

Take a look at the operations in your workteam in the last six months.

1 Identify TWO changes that have occurred during that time.

_____

_____

2 Identify what forces prompted the changes.

_____

_____

3 Identify who was responsible for making the financial case for that change.

_____

_____

4 Find out what sort of financial case was put forward for the changes. Were they coherently planned for and set out, or were they just 'allowed to happen'? If the latter was the case, what effect did this have on overall budgets and performance?

If you are compiling an S/NVQ portfolio you may be able to develop your notes into a full report recommending improvements in how changes are identified or how financial cases for change are put together. You may be able to use your report and feedback on it as the basis of possible acceptable evidence.

Self-assessment 1

15 mins

1 Fill in the missing words in the following sentence.

Organizations select ideas for projects if they have appropriate _____,

physical and financial _____ and if they have sufficient _____

to complete the project on schedule.

2 ■ Kitchen Caterers run the local school catering service for the county. Their contract is coming up for renewal and they and four other organizations are competing for the contract. Kitchen Caterers have a good reputation for quality of the food prepared, service and cleanliness and they charge premium prices to reflect the high quality.

Identify Kitchen Caterers':

■ Strength

_____

■ Weakness

_____

■ Opportunity

_____

■ Threat

_____

3 List the defined stages of the life cycles of products and services at which change may be useful.

_____

_____

_____

_____

4 Why is it important to allow for problems when planning projects?

_____

_____

5 Why are different criteria applied to unavoidable and to discretionary projects?

_____

_____

Answers to these questions can be found on pages 65–6.

7 Summary

- First line managers are well-placed to generate ideas for projects, but their implementation needs the support of more senior managers too.

- SWOT and PESTLE techniques are useful in identifying future projects so that the organization can make best use of its strengths and limit its weaknesses.

- Timing is very important. Change at crucial stages of the life cycle of products and services is likely to be most effective and these are appropriate times to make a case for change.

- It is important to think through potential consequences of investments and to build tolerances into plans for potential problems.

- Projects are selected for consideration which best fit the organization's:

  - experience;
  - physical and financial resources;
  - schedule of other commitments.

- Projects undertaken should aim to leave the organization as flexible as possible so that it can take advantage of future opportunities and not commit itself to onerous agreements.

Session B
Analysis of costs and benefits

1 Introduction

If you are thinking about buying a new car you will have a number of points in mind. Cost will be important, as will the condition of the car and its reliability. If you have a family and a dog you are likely to look for a different kind of car than if you are single. But once you have narrowed your choices to, say, three different cars, you will need specific measures to help you make the final choice. Price, fuel economy and servicing costs are likely to be important in your choice.

Money is also an important measure in organizations. There is little point in spending money on anything if it is not likely to bring in more money than it costs or if it does not provide other benefits to the organization. Financial considerations are important and various techniques are available to judge the potential financial success of projects.

Not all projects lead to profits, as we saw in Session A. For instance, a road cleaning machine will not earn money for a local authority but it will meet the organizational aims of improving the environment of the council tax payers and others. In situations like this, other measures are needed, which compare the costs of the project with the benefits that arise.

In this session we will look at different financial and other techniques for analysing the costs and benefits of projects. This involves looking at separate projects and the implications of projects for the organization as a whole.

First we will cover different ways of looking at the costs of projects, depending on whether the costs are committed already, or not, and are capital in nature or not.

2 Committed and discretionary costs

When you are considering a change which involves spending money in your workplace, it is important that you are clear about how much needs to be spent. If the change is inevitable you have no choice in what you have to spend, but at other times you have greater choice and flexibility.

Certain expenditure is required by the law and the requirements of the industry you work in.

Activity 12

3 mins

Think about your workplace. State **two** examples where changes involving expenditure have been required by legislation or industry standard rather than being decided upon by your organization.

_____

_____

There are a number of possibilities you may have suggested. Typically this required change will involve:

- health and safety equipment such as first-aid kit, machine guards, face masks, eye glasses;
- training costs associated with handling equipment safely;
- toilet and washing facilities and rest areas;
- removal of waste materials and cleaning.

The organization **must** spend money on these matters and they are known as **committed costs**.

You will still need to make some sort of financial case, because there are different ways of meeting such requirements, of course. For instance, waste disposal may be carried out by your organization or by using contractors. Such decisions have an impact on the overall cost but, nevertheless, some expenditure is still essential on these matters.

As a first line manager, it is important for you to ensure that your organization adheres to the law and industry standards, so you will find from time to time that you will need to update safety materials and so on. Although you will have a good chance of having your request for funds agreed, this could reduce the budget you have for other projects.

Organizations also have other committed costs and these arise when a decision has been taken to go ahead with a major change. For instance, say a decision has been made for your organization to operate from your workplace, which may be a single site or one of a number. The rent or mortgage paid for the work area is a committed cost because, to continue, your organization must continue to pay the monthly amount. Although it is not a statutory requirement to pay the rent or mortgage, the organization cannot continue its plans without meeting this commitment.

Other costs are **discretionary**, otherwise known as **managed** or **programmed** costs. Advertising is a good example because the amount of expenditure on advertising is completely under the control of the organization.

The total cost for any project is likely to be made up partly of committed and partly of discretionary costs.

Activity 13 · 3 mins

Katy Gorden is a first line manager in charge of a design office. She wishes to update the computers, mainly in preparation for the future time when her workteam will be required to undertake more complex design work. Katy says that she needs new computer equipment:

	Discretionary	Committed
so that it will be powerful enough to run new computer-aided design (CAD) programs	☐	☐
to meet current health and safety standards for computer screen emissions	☐	☐
to reduce 'down-time' because of faults with the existing equipment	☐	☐

Tick the cost(s) above which are discretionary and those which are committed.

You should have spotted that the health and safety requirements are likely to be **committed** costs. The expenditure on new equipment to reduce 'down-time' and to run new CAD programs would be **discretionary** in view of the situation described.

However, had Katy's team already been chosen to undertake more complex work, the computers needed to run more powerful programs would be essential and the costs would be committed rather than discretionary.

In the situation described in Activity 13, Katy has a good case for expenditure based on the changes needed for health and safety aspects. Committing expenditure to the replacement of computers would most likely be linked to the required implementation date for health and safety standards. But, if the organization had a need for new equipment within wider-ranging plans, it is likely that Katy would be given the go-ahead to spend money on the new computers earlier.

Have you been involved in situations like this? By understanding the overall plans and strategy of your organization, you will have a better idea of how likely you are to be successful in making the changes you need.

Now let us turn to an important distinction: between capital and revenue costs.

3 Capital and revenue costs

Most projects arising from changes require a certain amount of investment upfront – that is, they cost money initially, which we hope will be repaid over time by the project's benefits. When you are putting a financial case together, it is often this initial or **capital** outlay that will be at issue first.

What the capital cost actually comprises will depend on the project. Here are some common capital costs:

- new buildings, or lease premiums payable on buildings;
- new equipment, such as factory machinery, office or shop fixtures and fittings, computers, laboratory equipment and assembly robots;
- new vehicles, such as aeroplanes, ships, lorries, cars, and forklifts;
- site preparation, installation, initial training and software costs;

Activity 14 ·

5 mins

Say you are a first line manager in charge of opening a new shop selling ladies' clothing. What sort of capital costs would the project initially incur?

_____

_____

_____

_____

You probably thought of a number of items, such as the initial lease premium on the premises, the cost of refitting the shop (counters, fitting rooms, lights, décor, shopfront, security system), computer and point of sale equipment, and maybe a delivery van.

Clearly, the actual list of capital costs that a project will incur depends wholly on the nature of the project. The point to bear in mind is that they can often be more extensive than initially appears to be the case, and trying to quantify them for presentation in a financial case can be quite tricky.

Costs which are not incurred as the initial outlay but which do recur over time are classified as revenue costs. These are not only the day-to-day costs of, say, buying stock and selling it on (in the shop example) but also the costs of maintaining use of the capital items. On top of the capital cost of the lease premium, for instance, you will have to pay regular rent, which is a revenue cost.

Activity 15 ·

3 mins

Referring back to the situation in Activity 14, for each of the following items of initial capital cost, try to identify a related revenue cost which will be incurred over time.

Lights_____

Security system_____

Point of sale equipment_____

Delivery van_____

Lighting will require replacement bulbs over time, the security system will need maintaining, till rolls will be required by the point of sale equipment, and the van will need diesel.

3.1 Making savings

One of the most important reasons for distinguishing between capital and revenue items is that the former can generally be depreciated over time in the organization's accounts, whereas the latter is expensed immediately in the period in which it is incurred. We shall see the significance of this in the next section.

Another important reason is that, by incurring initial upfront capital costs, savings can be made on future revenue costs, which mean that, in total, the organization experiences a net cost saving.

An example of this is where a piece of machinery that costs £5,000 per year to maintain is replaced at a capital cost of £20,000, but annual maintenance costs are only £500. This is a revenue saving of £4,500 per year.

4 Payback period

This is probably the most frequently used technique for assessing the financial viability of projects. It regards projects which repay their capital cost most quickly as being best. For example, if a café purchases a new cooker for £1,000 and makes an average of £0.50 profit on each meal, the cooker will be paid for after £1,000/£0.50 = 2,000 meals. If the café sells 40 meals a day, the full price of the cooker is paid back after 2,000/40 = 50 days.

50 days is the payback period.

4.1 Use of the technique

Try the following Activity to apply the technique of payback period.

Activity 16

4 mins

Zoë and Hamid decided to set up a carpet cleaning business. They purchased carpet cleaning equipment for £800. On average they expect to earn £5 per carpet after expenses and to be able to clean two carpets a day, five days a week.

Calculate their payback period in weeks.

The payback period is

$$\frac{£800}{£5 \times 2 \times 5} = \frac{£800}{50} = 16 \text{ weeks}$$

You will appreciate as a first line manager that the calculations above are rather simplistic. The capital cost of equipment or machinery is fairly easy to work out. It is how much the organization paid for it together with delivery, installation and other costs incurred to get it up and running. But how is income calculated? And you know that income does not always flow in evenly.

4.2 Gathering information for analysis

In practice you will have a number of things to think about when making an analysis of costs and benefits. Gathering information is a very important skill.

Activity 17

10 mins

Hampdene Ltd is a company specializing in arable farming. It is thinking about purchasing a combine harvester for a capital cost of £160,000, to be used from August to early October on its fields. It will also be rented out to a neighbouring farm for the remainder of October.

Harvest income flows in from October to December and total sales are expected to bring in £60,000 in Year 1, £66,000 in Year 2 and £70,000 for each year from Year 3 to Year 8 (additional competition in world markets is faced in the later years). Running costs of the combine harvester are estimated at £4,000 a year for Year 1 and Year 2 and £5,000 for each year thereafter. Seeds, fertilizers and other costs of production are generally 50 per cent of the sales income.

Rental income from hiring out the vehicle is estimated at £2,000 per year for the foreseeable future.

While not in use, storage, security and maintenance expenses of the combine harvester are estimated at £1,000 per year.

Each year from Year 1 calculate the net income for the company generated from the use of the combine harvester, and complete the following table.

	Year 1 (£)	Year 2 (£)	Year 3 (£)	Year 4 (£)	Year 5 (£)	Year 6 (£)	Year 7 (£)	Year 8 (£)
Income								
crops (sales)								
rentals	2,000	2,000	2,000	2,000	2,000	2,000	2,000	2,000
Outgoings								
running costs								
storage, etc.								
cost of production of crop	____	____	____	____	____	____	____	____
Net income								

The combine harvester generates income from the sale of crops and from rentals. But certain revenue costs, such as storage, security, maintenance and running costs need to be paid, because without the combine harvester they would not be needed.

And not all the income from sale of crops should be seen as paying back the capital cost of the combine harvester because it must first pay back the cost of growing and planting. Without allowing for this, the company could not buy seeds and fertilizers for future years.

Your calculations of net income should be as follows.

	Year 1 (£)	Year 2 (£)	Year 3 (£)	Year 4 (£)	Year 5 (£)	Year 6 (£)	Year 7 (£)	Year 8 (£)
Income								
crops (sales)	60,000	66,000	70,000	70,000	70,000	70,000	70,000	70,000
rentals	2,000	2,000	2,000	2,000	2,000	2,000	2,000	2,000
	62,000	68,000	72,000	72,000	72,000	72,000	72,000	72,000
Outgoings								
running costs	4,000	4,000	5,000	5,000	5,000	5,000	5,000	5,000
storage, etc.	1,000	1,000	1,000	1,000	1,000	1,000	1,000	1,000
cost of production of crop	30,000	33,000	35,000	35,000	35,000	35,000	35,000	35,000
	35,000	38,000	41,000	41,000	41,000	41,000	41,000	41,000
Net income	27,000	30,000	31,000	31,000	31,000	31,000	31,000	31,000

Having put together the information you would be able to work out the payback period. But first, are there any other items of income or cost we have forgotten? Sometimes you will not have all the information you need and will have to ask for more.

Activity 18

3 mins

Note down three other financial costs or income items to Hampdene Ltd, which could be relevant.

_____

_____

_____

There are a number of other possible revenue costs you may have identified, although no further income appears to be available:

- insurance of the combine harvester;
- bank overdraft or loan interest if money is borrowed to buy the vehicle;
- any wages and salaries not already included in the expenses quoted. These would include the wage costs of planting and tending the crops and, as other equipment might be involved in these stages of production, you might need to

decide what proportion should be set against the combine harvester and how much against other equipment;

■ management overheads. Part of the cost of growing and selling crops and renting out the vehicle involves action by management;

■ depreciation of the combine harvester (over time the combine harvester will decline in value, and this needs to be recognized each year).

Many of the expenses are approximations. You cannot expect to calculate answers to the nearest £. The best you can hope for is a reasonable estimate.

These revenue costs, which are not always possible to attribute to a specific business activity but which arise from support which the business needs in order to operate, are known as **overheads**.

Having made sure that you have all the necessary information you can then calculate the payback period.

Activity 19 · 5 mins

Again referring to Hampdene Ltd, and assuming total overheads of £8,000 in Year 1, £7,000 in Year 2, £6,000 in Year 3, £5,000 in Year 4 and thereafter, calculate the payback period for the combine harvester up to and including Year 8.

The calculations for Year 1 and Year 2 are shown to start you off.

Year	Net income calculated (£)	*less*	Overheads (£)	=	Final net income (£)	Cost of combine harvester less final net income (£)
						(160,000)
Year 1	27,000	–	8,000	=	19,000	(141,000)
Year 2	30,000	–	7,000	=	23,000	(118,000)
Year 3						
Year 4						
Year 5						
Year 6						
Year 7						
Year 8						

The completed calculations are as follows. These show that the combine harvester 'pays back' in Year 7.

Year	Net income calculated (£)	less	Overheads (£)	=	Final net income (£)	Cost of combine harvester less final net income (£)
						(160,000)
Year 1	27,000	–	8,000	=	19,000	(141,000)
Year 2	30,000	–	7,000	=	23,000	(118,000)
Year 3	31,000	–	6,000	=	25,000	(93,000)
Year 4	31,000	–	5,000	=	26,000	(67,000)
Year 5	31,000	–	5,000	=	26,000	(41,000)
Year 6	31,000	–	5,000	=	26,000	(15,000)
Year 7	31,000	–	5,000	=	26,000	11,000
Year 8	31,000	–	5,000	=	26,000	37,000

Despite the obvious limitation of payback, it is widely used because it emphasizes how quickly cash flows into an organization. And cash is usually in short supply in organizations. Cash income which only occurs several years in the future is probably only of importance to stronger businesses which have a regular cash flow from operations and have less immediate concerns about additional cash.

Some firms have a set **cut-off point** or payback period of, say three years. Any project which does not produce payback of the initial capital cost within three years would not be looked at further. Clearly this eliminates good longer-term projects.

Payback is a useful cautious approach where it is particularly difficult to assess the future, such as where:

- projects are risky;
- the organization operates in uncertain markets;
- design and product changes occur rapidly.

Let's look at another common method of financial project appraisal – return on onvestment.

5 Return on investment

Return on investment, which you may also hear called **accounting rate of return** is a financial appraisal technique which tackles the problem that payback takes no account of income **after** the payback period. Return on investment looks at the overall income and expenditure over an entire project and is calculated as the:

$$\frac{\text{average annual project net profit}}{\text{average investment}} \times 100$$

How do you calculate the average investment. If a business purchased equipment for £8,000 with an expected four-year life and no projected scrap value at the end of its life, the average investment would be £8,000/4 = £2,000.

Assuming an average annual project net profit of £500 each year from the use of the equipment, the return on investment would be:

$$\frac{£500}{£2,000} \times 100 = 25\%$$

If an organization has a choice between investments, the one with the highest return on investment would be selected, using this method of financial appraisal.

Activity 20

Media Advertising Associates offer two advertising packages to their clients for advertising cosmetics:

- television and cinema advertising, which costs £1,000,000 annually and is likely to generate an average annual net profit of £140,000;
- newspaper, magazine and hoarding advertising, which costs £220,000 annually and is likely to generate an average annual net profit of £33,000.

Use the return on investment method to decide which is the best option for clients.

_____

_____

_____

_____

_____

_____

_____

_____

_____

The calculations for the two advertising packages are:

$$\text{Television etc.} \quad \frac{£140,000}{£1,000,000} \times 100 = 14\%$$

and

$$\text{Newspapers etc.} \quad \frac{£33,000}{£220,000} \times 100 = 15\%$$

The cheaper investment using newspapers, magazines and advertising hoardings represents better value for money.

However, if a client has £1,000,000 to spend, an additional £107,000 would be generated. The client must consider how the additional £780,000 investment would be spent otherwise. It might be more sensible to spend the higher amount to generate the higher income, unless other projects are available which would generate at least £107,000 from the 'spare' £780,000.

As with the payback method you can see that there are limitations to this method of appraisal too.

Let's now look at return on investment in more detail.

5.1 Profit-based measures

You will remember that payback period concentrates on cash. You deduct the net cash generated by an investment from its initial capital cost.

Return on investment is, instead, linked to profit-based measures. The main impact of this is that the cost of an investment is spread over the full period of its use. For example, if machinery costs £120,000 and is expected to have a five-year working life in the organization, after which it will be sold for £20,000, the total investment is regarded as £100,000 (£120,000 less £20,000). The average investment would be £20,000 each year for the five-year period (£100,000/5). Another way of looking at this annual investment in the machinery is as the worth of the machinery used up each year (depreciation). Depreciation is an expense deducted, like wages and salaries and heat and lighting, when calculating profit. Try the following activity so that you can compare payback method and return on investment.

Activity 21

5 mins

Henry bought a second-hand taxi for a capital cost of £13,000, which he expects to operate for three years, after which he should be able to sell it for £1,000. His projected earnings from fares over the three-year period are £8,000 per year after deducting expenses.

Complete the following to calculate payback period and return on investment.

	Payback		Return on investment	
	Yearly (£)	Total (£)		(£)
Beginning Purchase	(13,000)	(13,000)	Average annual net profit before depreciation	8,000
Year 1 Net income	8,000		Depreciation $\dfrac{(£13,000 - £1,000)}{3}$ (= Average investment)	_____
Year 2 Net income	8,000		Average annual net profit	_____
Year 3 Net income	8,000		$\dfrac{\text{Average annual net profit}}{\text{Average investment}} \times 100 = \underline{\quad} \times 100 = \quad \%$	
Year 3 Sale of taxi	1,000			

Your completed table, comparing the two approaches, should be as follows.

	Payback		Return on investment	
	Yearly (£)	Total (£)		(£)
Beginning Purchase	(13,000)	(13,000)	Average annual net profit before depreciation	8,000
Year 1 Net income	8,000	(5,000)	Depreciation $\dfrac{(£13,000 - £1,000)}{3}$ (= Average investment)	= 4,000
Year 2 Net income	8,000	3,000	Average annual net profit	4,000
Year 3 Net income	8,000	11,000	$\dfrac{\text{Average annual net profit}}{\text{Average investment}} \times 100 = \dfrac{£4,000}{£4,000} \times 100 = 100\%$	
Year 3 Sale of taxi	1,000	12,000		

Payback occurs in Year 2 and the rate of return is 100 per cent. There is no obvious connection between the two but, as you have calculated, the average annual net profit for each of the three years is £4,000, or £12,000 in total over the period. This is the same as the total generated after payback, if you follow the payback calculation through to the end of Year 3.

Organizations which use rate of return to appraise projects tend to have a cut-off point, as with the payback period. No project will be considered if the return on investment is below a certain level, say 40 per cent. If an organization has to borrow to finance a project, the rate of interest that the organization pays on the borrowing is the minimum possible return on investment that the organization could possibly consider without making a loss. And there is little point in an organization undertaking a project which will yield a lower return than would be generated by simply leaving money on deposit at the bank, with very little risk of loss.

Activity 22 · 5 mins

| S/NVQ A1.3, B1.1 |

This Activity may provide the basis of appropriate evidence for your S/NVQ portfolio. If you are intending to take this course of action, it might be better to write your answers on separate sheets of paper.

Find out the payback period and rate of return on investment used in your organization for projects. Make a note of these below for future reference.

Other popular methods of financial appraisal are **discounted cash flow (DCF)** and **internal rate of return**. Neither of these techniques are covered in this workbook but your ILM Centre will be able to advise you about books covering these topics if you wish to explore them.

■ Payback period

_____

■ Return on investment

_____

EXTENSION 3
Part 9 covers other techniques of financial appraisal.

Your answer is very dependent on the industry in which you work. If it is a high-tech or a risky area, required payback is likely to be short and return on investment high. If you are in a long-term and well-established industry with low risk, payback may be much longer and return on investment lower. Forestry, for example, requires growing trees over a long period so payback is, naturally, also over a long period. Some measure of risk analysis may be included in calculations and, for example, an estimate of risk added by an expectation of a generally higher rate of return to allow for riskier projects.

5.2 Information gathering

As with payback period, if you are to use the return on investment technique, you will need to be sure that you have gathered all relevant information on which to base your appraisal.

Typically, you will have certain information to hand and have to search out further details and think through the implications of options.

Activity 23 · 5 mins

Tony's workteam is involved in conservation work, which is financed by the local council, national grants and donations. Income is reducing from all sources because of external pressures so Tony has been asked to generate income from his workteam's activities.

There are a couple of possible ways of using the woodland managed by Tony and his team, in a sustainable way, which could generate money.

- Providing guided walks on certain themes, such as 'the morning chorus', 'colours of autumn', 'tracking for beginners' and so on. Specialist experts from local naturalist groups, whom Tony has talked to informally, have said that they would be available for a nominal fee of £10 each. The public could have limited free access to the woodland at other times. Tony feels that by charging £2 each for those wishing to go on the walks it would be easy to recover the cost of the guide. He expects an average of ten people on each walk and twenty-four walks a year.

- Using the wood gained from managing the woodland to make charcoal. This would involve an investment of £1,000 in equipment with a life of twenty years, and £200 to train and provide protective clothing for a couple of people to make the charcoal. This would then be sold for barbecues through local garden centres. Tony expects to be able to sell enough charcoal to provide an income of £600 a year.

Neither option would involve additional labour costs but new people would need to be trained and clothed for charcoal burning every year.

Calculate the return on investment over a three-year period.

How would you recommend Tony should proceed?

_____

_____

_____

_____

_____

_____

_____

_____

_____

Let's put together the information:

- The revenue cost of paying guides throughout a year would be 24 × £10 = £240. This would provide an income of 10 × £2 × 24 = £480 in a year. This gives a profit of £240 per year and £720 over the three-year period. The return on investment is:

$$\frac{£240}{£240} \times 100 = 100\%$$

- The equipment has an initial capital cost of £1,000 and lasts for twenty years which, assuming no scrap value for the equipment, requires depreciation of £1,000/20 = £50 to be charged each year. By adding this to training and clothing costs each year, the expenses of the charcoal burning option are £250. Income is estimated at £600 annually, so profit is £600 − £250 = £350 each year, and a total of £1,050 over three years. The return on investment is:

$$\frac{£350}{£250} \times 100 = 140\%$$

The charcoal burning option provides the greatest return on investment. Financially this appears to be the best option.

However, questions need to be asked before advising Tony which option to take.

- Does Tony have any other options which should be included in a full appraisal of the situation? For instance, is there another market for the wood, such as providing small garden fencing or bark mulch for gardens?
- Does Tony have £1,200 cash to spend on charcoal burning equipment and training? The first option of guided tours provided immediate payback so long as five people or more attend the first walk. It takes nearly three years to achieve payback on the charcoal burning equipment. If he does spend £1,200, does this limit what else his workteam can do?
- Can only one option be undertaken or is it possible to do both? The guided walk option seems, financially, only to require the risk of £10 on each occasion to pay the guide.
- How certain is Tony about his figures and the markets? It is essential that the charcoal could be sold for three years to repay the initial cost of the equipment. But will people still require barbecue charcoal in ten to twenty years time? If not, is there another market for charcoal? Guided tours are far less risky financially.

You may also have thought of matters other than purely financial ones.

- Is it acceptable environmentally to take people through the woodland twenty-four times a year on tours? Will this damage the environment?

■ Will charcoal burning damage the environment and cause pollution for, say, local farmers and villages?

■ If Tony wishes to run both charcoal burning and guided tours, will the charcoal burning activities reduce (or increase) the number of people who take the guided tours?

It is difficult to measure the cost of such points but, particularly in the public sector, such matters do need to be thought about.

The technique of cost-benefit analysis itself is used as a way of trying to measure the impact of such matters in an overall appraisal of projects.

6 Non-financial cost-benefit analysis

The technique of cost-benefit analysis attempts to identify and quantify the non-financial costs and benefits of a project. For instance, if a county council wants to put a by-pass around a village, it will be able to calculate the capital costs of building the road in terms of labour and tarmac. But there are other costs associated with the by-pass, some of which are non-financial:

■ maintenance costs;
■ pollution from exhaust fumes and dirt;
■ water pollution from a mixture of rain and rubber, heavy metals and so on, which accumulate on the road through use, as the mixture runs off into ditches and fields;
■ noise;
■ loss of green fields;
■ general damage to the landscape.

There are benefits, though:

■ savings in journey time;
■ fewer accidents;
■ better quality of life for villagers along the existing road;
■ fewer large commercial vehicles may replace an extra number of smaller ones previously needed to handle smaller village roads.

Activity 24

2 mins

Select one cost and one benefit of the by-pass project discussed above. How would you place a value on the effects?

_____

_____

_____

Some costs, such as maintenance, are financial in nature and can be estimated in monetary terms by including potential material and labour costs. Pollution is more difficult to quantify, but you can measure the costs of cleaning up pollution in the village over a few years. You can find a similar by-pass in another part of the country and work out the costs associated with cleaning up pollution there over a similar period. This provides a monetary measure of improved conditions along the road in the village against the worsened conditions along the by-pass.

Savings in travelling time for people could, perhaps, be linked to an average rate of pay per hour as a typical measure of their time.

The cost of accidents can be measured by the costs of treating the victims in hospital. Any resulting deaths can also be given a monetary value by reference to the actuarial tables used in the insurance industry to estimate the likely life span of individuals. There is then the problem of putting a value on each person and their likely contribution to the community.

Even more difficult to put a monetary value on is a view over a landscape. But if you buy a house which looks out over rolling downland, you would expect to pay more for it than for a similar house with a view of the local gasworks. So that gives a basis on which to make some estimation.

Of course, the above measures are purely estimates and someone who works for Friends of the Earth will put a different value on the environment than would a land developer.

Activity 25 · 2 mins

S/NVQ A1.3, B1.1

This Activity may provide the basis of appropriate evidence for your S/NVQ portfolio. If you are intending to take this course of action, it might be better to write your answers on separate sheets of paper.

Do you use cost-benefit analysis at work when appraising projects? How far does your organization go in trying to put a value on matters which are not easily measured in financial terms? If applicable, give **two** examples.

If your organization does not use cost-benefit analysis, think about a recent project at work and say how you would have valued non-financial aspects related to the project.

_____

_____

Much depends on the view of your organization about cost-benefit analysis. Some consider that social costs cannot be measured with certainty, so it is not logical to try to put a monetary value on them. Others take social costs and benefits into consideration as well as making a financial appraisal, but take a subjective approach. Some people try to put a clear monetary value on such matters, for instance linking time saved to an average wage. Costs measured in this way are known as **shadow prices**.

6.1 Externalities

Acid rain is an example of an externality which crosses international boundaries and cannot be linked to specific producers. Perhaps a country could be made to compensate?

Externalities are the effects that organizations have on society. Conventional accounting does not recognize the costs of, say, discharging toxic waste into a river. The government has a policy of 'the polluter pays' so the charge for cleaning up the waste is passed on by the water companies or the appropriate agency to the polluter. This is a social cost with a clearly defined price and is a useful basis for a shadow price. But if the polluter cannot be identified the public funds pick up the bill.

Externalities can also be social benefits. A new factory in an area of high unemployment not only provides jobs and income for employees. It also removes the need for unemployment and other benefits to be paid to individuals and families. This is the social benefit.

Activity 26 ·

30 mins

This Activity may provide the basis of appropriate evidence for your S/NVQ portfolio. If you are intending to take this course of action, it might be better to write your answers on separate sheets of paper.

Select an item of equipment or machinery in your workplace which will need replacement soon. Find out the capital cost of two possible replacements and discuss with your manager the income and profits likely to be generated by the replacements, together with their potential life.

1 Prepare a financial appraisal of the replacements, using the payback period and return on investment techniques.

2 Undertake a cost-benefit analysis of the new machinery or equipment compared with the present situation.

3 Choose the preferable option and say why.

_____

_____

_____

_____

_____

_____

_____

_____

_____

_____

_____

If you are compiling an S/NVQ portfolio you may be able to develop your notes into a full report recommending selection of new machinery or equipment to provide to management. You may be able to use your report and feedback on it as the basis of possible acceptable evidence.

As you or your manager may actually have to undertake this task, you are more likely to receive help if you give details of your investigation to your manager and save your organization time.

Your choice and options for replacements suggested depend on the industry in which you work.

However, you are likely to have identified a number of financial and other benefits and costs:

- tangible costs (capital or revenue) – can be quantified in monetary terms, such as the cost of equipment or services;
- non-recurring costs – comprise capital costs of equipment, site preparation, initial studies, software conversion, one-off training on the new equipment, cost of reallocating human resources, contractual and support services;
- recurring revenue costs – are paid throughout the life of the project and comprise rentals, leases, licence fees, wages and salaries, travel and ongoing training costs, maintenance and support services;
- intangible costs – such as efficiency loss during training on the new project;
- tangible benefits – such as income generated from the new equipment and avoidance of costs previously incurred;
- non-recurring benefits – comprising operational effectiveness and saving of resources;
- recurring benefits – comprising operational effectiveness and saving of resources;
- intangible benefits – like improved service to the public, improved accuracy and delivery times, better control and security, productivity savings.

Self-assessment 2

15 mins

1 Calculate the payback period for the following.

- Chan Kam Wan invested £2,000 from her budget in equipment to reduce wastage in her work area. In the first year this saved her organization £600 and £800 each year after.

2 ■ Paris Ltd bought machinery for £10,000 with a life of five years and no scrap value. Before depreciation the profit generated by the machinery was £3,000. Calculate the return on investment.

_____

_____

_____

_____

_____

3 Complete the following by filling in the missing words.

Some costs and benefits are easily measured financially. Others are less tangible and measured through the use of _____ _____ analysis. One way of putting a price on such intangibles is by using _____ prices.

4 Identify whether the following examples are tangible or intangible costs, tangible or intangible benefits.

a cost of equipment _____ _____

b productivity savings _____ _____

c avoidance of costs _____ _____

d efficiency loss _____ _____ .

Answers to these questions can be found on page 66.

7 Summary

- The total cost of projects usually comprises committed and discretionary costs.

- Committed costs are required by legislation and industry standards and cannot usually be avoided.

- Discretionary costs are controlled by the organization.

- Capital costs are incurred by the organization on the initial outlay on a project.

- Revenue costs are incurred over time.

- Payback and return on investment are financial appraisal methods commonly used.

- Payback selects projects by regarding the best option as being the project which returns its capital cost the most quickly. It is particularly useful where:

  - projects are risky;
  - the organization operates in uncertain markets;
  - design and product changes occur rapidly.

- Payback does not consider income after the payback period.

- Return on investment looks at the overall income and expenditure over an entire project and rates projects according to their level of return.

- Return on investment is calculated using the formula:

$$\frac{\text{average annual net profit}}{\text{average investment}} \times 100$$

- Payback uses cash measures and return on investment makes calculations through profit-based measures.

- Return on investment rejects investments with a potential return under a given cut-off point.

- Some costs and benefits are more difficult to measure and cost-benefit analysis is used to approve these. Shadow prices are sometimes used to put a financial measure on intangible costs and benefits.

- Cost-benefit analysis sets out to measure externalities and is used in conjunction with financial analysis techniques to assess projects.

Session C
Presenting a financial case

1 Introduction

'Hey pal. Gi' me a fiver for a cab!'

'Excuse me, I'm really sorry to trouble you. I wouldn't if I didn't have to. Oh, I hate doing this. You must think I'm really awful. You see I had my money stolen. I had it when I left home this morning. I remember because I counted it when I was coming to work this morning on the bus . . .'

'Could I please borrow £2.50 to get the bus home tonight? I've lost my money and haven't a penny left. I will pay you back tomorrow morning.'

There are many different ways to ask for money. Which one of the above do you prefer? I hope you will agree that you the best approach is the straightforward one, which provides you with a good reason for the request, does not waste your time and states how and when you will get your money back.

In the first two sessions you developed your ability to evaluate projects and decide between options. If you wish to see your projects implemented, you need to obtain agreement from management to go ahead and therefore, to give your projects the best chance to be selected, you must be able to present a case well.

When you are presenting a financial case for a project to go ahead, remember this. Be clear, precise and give appropriate factual details for:

- the money needed;
- why it is needed;
- how it will benefit the organization;
- how the investment is to be repaid.

Your organization may want a slightly different approach from other organizations but the general principles are common and we will look at these in this session.

2 The right presentation

Your organization may have its own forms on which requests for finance must be made. Or an unofficial set pattern may have been arrived at by people following a given pattern some time ago.

Activity 27 · 5 mins

Think about expensive purchases you have made personally or have been involved in making for your organization. Suggest the various key points you have needed to consider and that you would expect to see included in the documents of request for finance.

_____

_____

_____

_____

_____

_____

_____

Your suggestions are likely to have included:

- the amount needed;
- what it is needed for and why it is needed now;
- the way the investment will benefit the organization;
- the way the investment is to be financed;
- the payback or return on investment.

Detailed calculations, cost-benefit justifications and further explanations typically complete the documentation. It is important to know who is going to receive the report or request. You may know them or of them. How will they react if a request for finance conforms or does not conform to this presentation? Your understanding of this will help you judge how you should complete your financial cases to ensure you are successful in your requests wherever possible.

3 Gathering information

There is usually quite a lot involved in putting together a financial case and it takes time. Because of this a useful preliminary start is to discuss your ideas with your manager before putting together a formal case. This will identify any problems early and your manager may be able to provide useful suggestions, such as the right time to present the case to senior management. Once you have the preliminary agreement from your manager, you are less likely to encounter objections later, although, of course, if your analysis of the appraisal identifies that the project will not be viable, your manager is unlikely to encourage it being taken further.

So, the stages of getting a project up and running are:

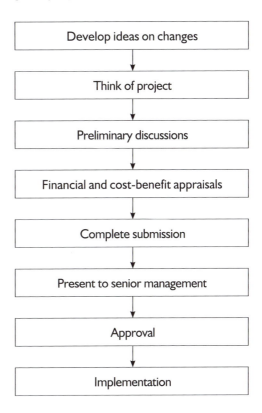

Considerable information is needed at different stages. The following diagram looks at the stages you will follow in selecting information for the right project.

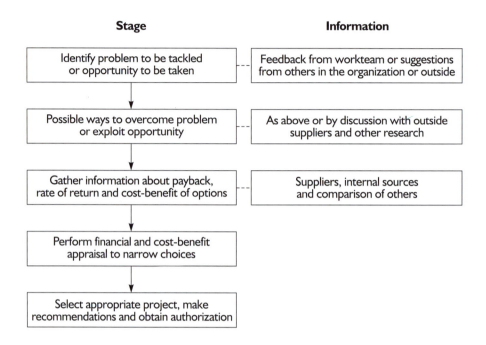

Stage	**Information**
Identify problem to be tackled or opportunity to be taken	Feedback from workteam or suggestions from others in the organization or outside
Possible ways to overcome problem or exploit opportunity	As above or by discussion with outside suppliers and other research
Gather information about payback, rate of return and cost-benefit of options	Suppliers, internal sources and comparison of others
Perform financial and cost-benefit appraisal to narrow choices	
Select appropriate project, make recommendations and obtain authorization	

Information gathering is very important early on. It is an important stage in the process and is less expensive than implementing the project itself. Perhaps the most difficult part of the process is identifying appropriate projects, although the need for some change will always eventually occur.

Activity 28 ·

6 mins

Hall and Deacon Ltd is a firm of printers which has run a successful local business for some years producing letterheads and other business stationery.

In recent years business has dropped off and several potential customers have commented that the company's charges are high and designs are not as flexible as those available from competitors who use electronic and disk-to-print equipment.

The company has not made changes in its existing equipment because:

- it paid back its cost ten years ago and the business makes a return on investment of 25 per cent each year;
- new equipment on the market continually needs updating and always seems to be going out of date, so there seems little point in changing until it is essential.

If you worked for this organization would you consider presenting a case for change and, if so, what information would you need?

_____

_____

_____

_____

_____

_____

_____

_____

It is likely to be difficult to get any financial case agreed in the light of the overall view taken by the organization. But that does not mean you should not try. Any manager has a responsibility to make suggestions to improve organizational effectiveness.

Although waiting until change is essential may have financial merits, the company will have no experience of new technology and may find it difficult to go straight into using sophisticated equipment.

Information you would need includes:

- details of optional projects, their capital and ongoing revenue costs and full details of possible additional work which might be gained by the company;
- details of expected future changes so that the life of new equipment can be judged.

The business is unlikely to accept anything which would yield a return on investment of less than 25 per cent.

Has this led you to think about any potential changes in your organization?

Activity 29 ·

20 mins

S/NVQ A1.3, B1.1

This Activity may provide the basis of appropriate evidence for your S/NVQ portfolio. If you are intending to take this course of action, it might be better to write your answers on separate sheets of paper.

Identify a situation at work where you feel change is appropriate. Investigate possible ways in which changes could be made and perform payback and return on investment techniques and cost-benefit analysis on possible projects.

Decide whether change really is appropriate and which project you prefer.

Make notes of your findings.

_____

_____

_____

_____

_____

_____

_____

_____

_____

_____

_____

_____

_____

_____

_____

_____

_____

If you are compiling an S/NVQ portfolio you may be able to develop your notes into a full report about change to provide to management. You may be able to use your report and feedback on it as the basis of possible acceptable evidence.

Once you have details and have made your decisions you then need to present your case.

4 Submitting the financial case

Once you have drawn up the case your organization will require it to be presented in the right way.

Activity 30

S/NVQ B1.1

This Activity may provide the basis of appropriate evidence for your S/NVQ portfolio. If you are intending to take this course of action, it might be better to write your answers on separate sheets of paper.

Examine any instructions about presenting financial cases in organizational manuals and discuss procedures with managers. Make notes about what you learn and draw up a report format indicating the typical headings you would be expected to include to meet the needs of your organization.

_____

_____

_____

_____

_____

_____

_____

If you are compiling an S/NVQ portfolio you may be able to use what you have learnt from this activity in preparing reports for management; you may be able to use your report and feedback on it as the basis of possible acceptable evidence.

Every organization is different and the more you know about how to approach senior managers with requests, the easier you will make your own life and the more effective you will be for your organization as a whole.

Self-assessment 3 · 10 mins

1 List the eight key stages in getting a project up and running.

_____

_____

_____

_____

_____

_____

_____

_____

2 Complete the following:

It is important to gather full information to ensure that an appropriate _____ is selected to overcome a problem. Choices are narrowed by performing _____ analysis and _____ _____ analysis.

3 Complete the following:

Using the appropriate forms of submission is more likely to mean that your request for finance will be _____. Familiarity helps senior _____ to examine the _____ effectively.

4 Select the appropriate response from the following choices:

When presenting a case for finance, which of the following need to be included?

A How much money is needed.
B How successful the organization has been in the past.
C How comprehensive the selection of projects has been.
D How the project benefits the organization.

Tick one of the following options.

A and B ☐
B and C ☐
C and D ☐
A and D ☐

Answers to these questions can be found on page 67.

5 Summary

- When presenting a case for finance, important details are:

  - the money needed;
  - why it is needed;
  - how it will benefit the organization;
  - how the investment is to be repaid.

- A financial case needs to be:

  - clearly presented;
  - easy to understand;
  - in a form which makes the most effective use of everyone's time.

- Gathering information is an important stage in putting together a financial case. Comprehensive information means that more aspects of a project can be considered and there is less chance of money being spent unwisely.

Performance checks

1 Quick quiz

Jot down your answers to the following questions on *Making a Financial Case*.

Question 1 Why are first line managers in good positions to identify changes in the organization?

_____

Question 2 What does SWOT analysis examine?

_____

_____

_____

Question 3 What does a PESTLE analysis consider?

_____

_____

_____

Question 4 List the four stages of a product life cycle where change is regularly considered.

_____

Question 5 Give another name for managed costs.

_____

Question 6   What is the difference between capital and revenue costs?

_____

_____

_____

Question 7   Name the financial technique which values most highly projects that repay their investment early.

_____

Question 8   Which financial appraisal technique gives the highest priority to projects that generate the most money from a given investment?

_____

Question 9   What are the two different bases of measurement used in investment appraisal techniques?

_____

_____

_____

Question 10   What is meant by a cut-off point in financial investment appraisal?

_____

_____

Question 11   What does cost-benefit analysis set out to do?

_____

_____

_____

Question 12   How are monetary values given to social benefits and costs?

_____

_____

_____

Question 13   State the four important details that need to be included in a financial case for a project.

_____

_____

Answers to these questions can be found on pages 67–8.

2 Workbook assessment

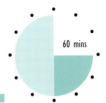

60 mins

Read the following case incident and then deal with the questions that follow. Write your answers on a separate sheet of paper.

> Sam is a first line manager in a despatch department of an organization which has put more emphasis on its mail order business in the last couple of years.
>
> Two members of Sam's workteam are due to retire shortly and Sam has seen equipment in a trade magazine which could be run by one person and could do the work of four. Sam sees this as being a way of dealing with an increased workload without taking on extra staff. It also uses plastic covering rather than cardboard, at a reduced cost for packaging.
>
> The equipment will cost £30,000 and should have a working life of six years at least. A further £3,000 will be needed to train up several staff to be able to work it effectively but, once the initial training period is over, no further training costs should be necessary over the following six years.
>
> The brochure about the equipment suggests that it will generate £15,000 profit for the organization before depreciation each year. Sam has worked out that it will save £500 a month for the organization before taking into account the reduced wages bill after the retirement of staff.
>
> The total present wages bill for the two staff who are due to retire is £24,000 a year.

1 Calculate the payback period for the equipment.

2 Calculate the return on investment.

3 Comment on any other non-financial costs and benefits that Sam should consider.

4 Explain whether you would recommend that Sam's organization should purchase this equipment. If so, justify your decision. If not, suggest what other options, if any, are available.

3 Work-based assignment

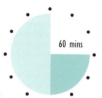

60 mins

The time guide for this assignment gives you an approximate idea of how long it is likely to take you to write up your findings. You will need to spend some additional time gathering information, perhaps talking to your manager and colleagues and thinking about the assignment. As you research and report, you should aim to develop your personal competency too. Ensure that you talk to people at mutually acceptable times, so that the information you receive is of the best quality and that people are fully committed to helping you. You may need to convince them of the value of your work, for instance. The result of your efforts should be presented on separate sheets of paper.

What you have to do

1 Talk to your manager to find out what investments need to be made in the short term and suggest that you would like to develop a case for an investment.

2 Draw up a case for the investment.

   a Obtain as much financial and cost-benefit information as possible about the potential investment.
   b Draw up a financial appraisal, using both payback period and return on investment techniques. Add a full cost-benefit analysis.
   c Analyse your figures and other information, comparing any choices you have.

3 Arrange to present your preliminary findings to your manager, making a note of any helpful suggestions towards presenting your case. If this is not possible, prepare a similar report on a suitable investment to your manager or trainer and discuss your findings.

Reflect and review

1 Reflect and review

Now that you have completed your work on *Making a Financial Case*, let us review our workbook objectives.

You should be better able to:

■ understand the ways in which changes and ideas develop into projects.

■ What changes have been experienced in your work area? What successes does your workteam have in implementing new projects?

_____

_____

_____

_____

■ It is important to understand the aims of your organization when making financial cases. What does your organization look for in viable projects?

_____

_____

_____

_____

■ In assessing viability, organizations need to consider experience, available time and resources, and ideas for projects should be generated with such matters in mind. Can you think of three or four projects which would improve the situation of your workteam and organization? (Perhaps SWOT and PESTLE techniques will help you.) Make a note of these.

_____

_____

_____

_____

_____

The second workbook objective was to:

■ use techniques to appraise investment.

Organizations use different methods to appraise projects and we looked at payback period and return on investment in this workbook.

As a first line manager, you may be involved in making a case for an investment or in collecting information for an investment appraisal. Think about your present role and make a note of anything else you can do to assist in effective appraisal.

■ Cost-benefit analysis techniques may also be relevant to your organization. What are the areas that need to be included in such an appraisal?

_____

_____

_____

_____

_____

_____

The final workbook objective was to:

■ prepare a financial case.

It is important to present a clear and straightforward case in the best way. Perhaps you have a better idea now of what needs to be included in a good financial case.

■ List the key requirements below so that you can use the best approach in future.

_____

_____

_____

_____

_____

2 Action plan

Use this plan to further develop for yourself a course of action you want to take. Make a note in the left-hand column of the issues or problems you want to tackle, and then decide what you intend to do and make a note in column 2.

The resources you need might include time, materials, information or money. You may need to negotiate for some of them, but they could be something easily acquired, like half an hour of somebody's time, or a chapter of a book. Put whatever you need in column 3. No plan means anything without a timescale, so put a realistic target completion date in column 4.

Finally, describe the outcome you want to achieve as a result of this plan, whether it is for your own benefit or advancement, or a more efficient way of doing things.

Desired outcomes			
1 Issues	2 Action	3 Resources	4 Target completion
Actual outcomes			

3 Extensions

Extension 1

Book   *Exploring Corporate Strategy*
Authors   Kevan Scholes and Gerry Johnson
Edition   Sixth, 2001
Publisher   FT Prentice Hall

Extension 2

Book   *Essential Managers 12: Managing Change*
Author   Robert Heller
Edition   1998
Publisher   Dorling Kindersley

Extension 3

Book   *Frank Wood's Business Accounting 2*
Authors   Frank Wood, Alan Sangster (Editor)
Edition   9th edition, 2002
Publisher   FT Prentice Hall

These extensions can be taken up via your ILM Centre. They will either have them or will arrange that you have access to them. However, it may be more convenient to check out the materials with your personnel or training people at work – they may well give you access. There are other good reasons for approaching your own people: for example, they will become aware of your interest and you can involve them in your development.

4 Answers to self-assessment questions

Self-assessment 1 on page 19

1 Organizations select ideas for projects if they have appropriate **EXPERIENCE**, physical and financial **RESOURCES** and if they have sufficient **TIME** to complete the project on schedule.

2   Kitchen Caterers':

- strength is good reputation for service;
- weakness is cost;
- opportunity is the contract for renewal;
- threat is the competition.

3   The stages of the life cycle are: introduction, growth, maturity, decline.

4   It is important to allow for problems to avoid additional costs later and to make contingency plans to avoid major disruption.

5   There is no question of choosing to undertake an unavoidable project, while there are a number of criteria which should be applied before undertaking a discretionary project.

Self-assessment 2 on page 43

1   Payback occurs in the third year of use as shown below.

		Annually (£)	Total (£)
Year 0	Purchase	2,000	(2,000)
Year 1	Savings	600	(1,400)
Year 2	Savings	800	(600)
Year 3	Savings	800	200

2   The return on investment is:

$$\frac{£1,000}{£2,000} \times 100 = 50\%$$

Depreciation is £10,000/5 = £2,000, which is the average annual investment.

The average profit less depreciation is £3,000 − £2,000 = £1,000.

3   Some costs and benefits are easily measured financially. Others are less tangible and measured through the use of **COST-BENEFIT** analysis. One way of putting a price on such intangibles is by using **SHADOW** prices.

4   The items can be categorized as follows:

a   cost of equipment – tangible cost
b   productivity savings – intangible benefit
c   avoidance of costs – tangible benefit
d   efficiency loss – intangible cost

Self-assessment 3 on page 54

1 The key stages in getting a project up and running are:

- develop ideas on changes;
- think of a project;
- have preliminary discussions;
- do financial and cost-benefit appraisals;
- complete submission;
- present to senior management;
- get approval;
- implement.

2 It is important to gather full information to ensure that an appropriate **PROJECT** is selected to overcome a problem. Choices are narrowed by performing **FINANCIAL** analysis and **COST-BENEFIT** analysis.

3 Using the appropriate forms of submission is more likely to mean that your request for finance will be **SUCCESSFUL**. Familiarity helps senior **MANAGEMENT** to examine the **PROJECT** effectively.

4 'A and D' is the correct answer. An organization needs to know how much it will have to commit financially and knowing how a project will benefit the organization aids overall management appraisal. Previous successes of the organization may have built up retained profits, say, but have no relevance to the future. Although selecting projects is important, management are concerned with relevant cases put before them, not all the projects that have been rejected at an early stage.

5 Answers to the quick quiz

Answer 1 Because they are in close contact with employees, customers, suppliers and competitors.

Answer 2 Organizational Strengths, Weaknesses, Opportunities and Threats.

Answer 3 Political, Economic, Social, Technological, Legal and Environmental factors.

Answer 4 Introduction, growth, maturity, decline.

Answer 5 Discretionary costs.

Answer 6   Capital costs are a projects initial outlay; revenue costs are incurred over time.

Answer 7   Payback period.

Answer 8   Return on investment.

Answer 9   Cash based and profit based.

Answer 10   The maximum payback period or minimum return on investment that an organization will accept.

Answer 11   Identify and quantify social costs and benefits.

Answer 12   By using shadow prices.

Answer 13   The money needed, why it is needed, how it benefits the organization and how the investment is repaid.

6 Certificate

Completion of this certificate by an authorized person shows that you have worked through all the parts of this workbook and satisfactorily completed the assessments. The certificate provides a record of what you have done that may be used for exemptions or as evidence of prior learning against other nationally certificated qualifications.

Pergamon Flexible Learning and ILM are always keen to refine and improve their products. One of the key sources of information to help this process are people who have just used the product. If you have any information or views, good or bad, please pass these on.

INSTITUTE OF LEADERSHIP & MANAGEMENT
SUPERSERIES

Making a Financial Case

....

has satisfactorily completed this workbook

Name of signatory ....

Position ....

Signature ....

Date ....

Official stamp

Fourth Edition

INSTITUTE OF LEADERSHIP & MANAGEMENT

SUPERSERIES

FOURTH EDITION

To order – phone us direct for prices and availability details
(please quote ISBNs when ordering) on 01865 888190